MONEY BASICS

SAVING AND INVESTING

by Martha London

BrightPoint Press

San Diego, CA

BrightPoint Press

an imprint of ReferencePoint Press, Inc.
Printed in the United States

For more information, contact:
BrightPoint Press
PO Box 27779
San Diego, CA 92198
www.BrightPointPress.com

LIBRARY OF CONGRESS CATALOGING-IN-PUBLICATION DATA

Names: London, Martha, author.
Title: Saving and investing / by Martha London.
Description: San Diego, CA : ReferencePoint Press, [2020] | Series: Money basics | Includes bibliographical references and index. | Audience: Grades 10-12.
Identifiers: LCCN 2019034006 (print) | LCCN 2019034007 (eBook) | ISBN 9781682828014 (hardcover) | ISBN 9781682828021 (eBook)
Subjects: LCSH: Saving and investment--Juvenile literature. | Finance, Personal--Juvenile literature.
Classification: LCC HB822 .L66 2020 (print) | LCC HB822 (eBook) | DDC 332.024--dc23
LC record available at https://lccn.loc.gov/2019034006
LC eBook record available at https://lccn.loc.gov/2019034007

CONTENTS

INTRODUCTION

LOOKING TO THE FUTURE

Sam's parents sit at the dinner table. A woman sits on the other side. She has a briefcase. It has many sheets of paper. Some of the papers are spread on the table. The woman is a financial **advisor**. She helps Sam's parents make good choices with their money. Today she is helping Sam's parents invest their money.

Financial advisors explain the options people have to save and invest their money.

Sam is at the kitchen counter nearby. He listens to his parents and the financial advisor. Sam is in high school. His parents are not retiring yet. But they will someday.

They want to be ready. Part of being ready means having enough money. They are meeting with the financial advisor to make sure they are on the right track.

Sam has a part-time job. He works at a grocery store after school. Sam's parents told him it is important to save money. If he saves money, he can buy things he needs. When Sam needed a car, he saved his money. Sam bought a used car. Now he is saving for college. College **tuition** is expensive. Sam will need to work. But he hopes he can take out fewer **loans** because he has savings.

The average public college tuition for the 2019–2020 school year was $10,116. It was $36,801 for private colleges. Students often start saving money for college in high school.

The woman shows Sam's parents some options. There are different stocks they can buy. They can also buy bonds. Or they can invest in a mutual fund.

It's good to save money in case there is an emergency, such as car trouble.

Sam reminds himself to ask his parents about these options later. Each option has pros and cons. Some have high **interest** rates. Others are less likely to lose money.

Some earn more money but are riskier. The woman says it is important to have a mix of investments.

SAVING AND INVESTING

Saving money is important. People need money for emergencies. They also need to be able to make large purchases. People do not want to work for their whole lives. Saving and investing allows people to retire.

Saving and investing are similar. But they are not the same. People use savings and investments for different things. Starting to save early is important. Saving and investing are great ways to plan for the future.

CHAPTER ONE

WHAT ARE SAVING AND INVESTING?

People save and invest for the future. They save and invest to prepare for emergencies. Some experts say a person "should aim to have a nest egg of $1 million to $1.5 million [to retire]." They also say that "your savings should amount to 10 to 12 times your current income."[1] But there is no

Saving and investing help people prepare for the near and distant future.

perfect amount for everyone to aim for. The amount that people should save and invest depends on their life situations. Saving and investing help people live comfortably. But each serves a different purpose.

People decide how much money to save and invest. Their decisions depend on what they want to do with their money. There are many different ways to save and invest. Each option has pros and cons.

SAVING

People save when they set money aside. They plan to spend this money in the future. There are many ways for people to save their money. Savings accounts are one popular option. They keep savings separate from spending money. People set up savings accounts through banks. Banks can use the money elsewhere. For example,

Opening a savings account with a bank is a good way to store money. Money can be taken out at any time.

they can loan it out to other people. Because banks use the money, they typically pay interest. Interest is a fee that is paid to the person who owns the money. This means that the money in the account will grow over time.

The Difference Between Saving and Investing

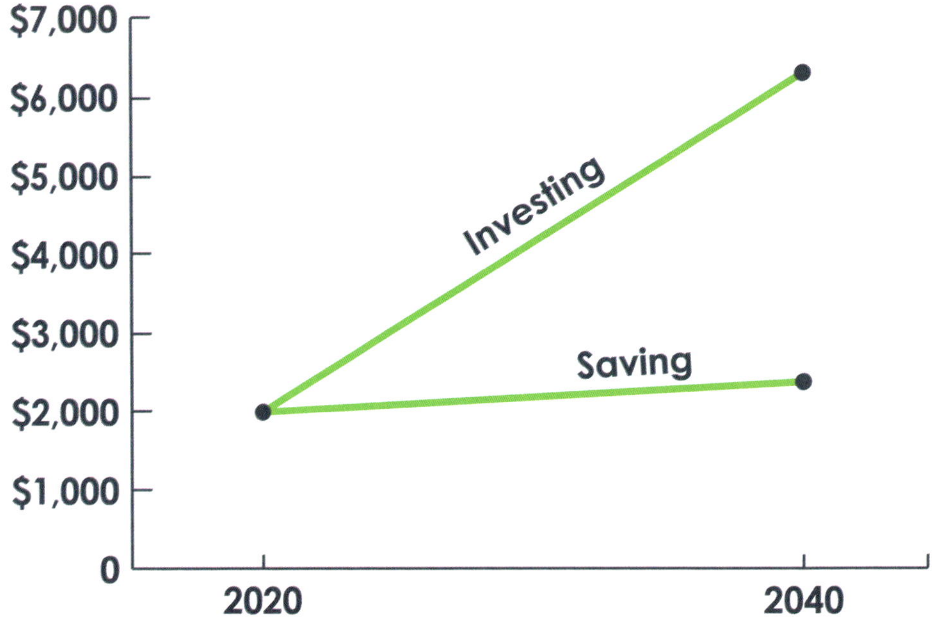

Say a person put $2,000 in a savings account at 1 percent annual interest. In twenty years, it would grow to $2,443 (before taxes). Another person invested $2,000 in a stock mutual fund. The fund earned an average of 6 percent per year. In twenty years, the investment would grow to $6,414 (before taxes). That is a difference of $3,971.

Savings accounts allow people to access their money easily. People can take money out at any time. This is important if there is an unexpected **expense**. Savings accounts are meant to hold on to money. There are often limits on how many times people can **withdraw** money each month. If people withdraw money too many times, there may be a **penalty**.

Savings accounts are also a low-risk option. Savings are insured by the government. This means the government

UNDER THE MATTRESS?

A 2015 study showed that many people hide their money. This is unwise. It is safer to have money in a bank. Money in a bank is protected. The government insures the money. Banks also provide interest on savings. Money in a home could be stolen or destroyed in a fire or flood.

will pay back a certain amount of money that is lost. But savings accounts have low interest rates. A low interest rate means the money in the account earns little. Saving is a great first step in preparing for the future.

INVESTING

Like saving, investing helps a person gain money over time. Investing means putting money into something that will be worth more later. Investments become more valuable over time. Most investments last many years. When people invest, they expect their money to grow. For example, people may invest money in land.

People keep track of their investments to see if they are making or losing money.

They expect the land to be worth more later. When they sell the land, they earn more money than they put into it. They get a return on their investment. A return is the money a person makes from an investment. Many people invest their money in businesses. They buy stocks. Stocks are small pieces of companies. They are worth more when a company does well. People can buy and sell these stocks to earn more money.

INVESTING RISKS

Investing is riskier than saving. Investments may lose value. For example, land's price may drop. Businesses may do poorly. If there is a downturn in the economy, the prices of stocks fall. The economy can also affect the prices of land. A low price means the investment is worth less money. However, investments are almost always kept for a long time. Waiting to sell investments gives the economy time to recover. As the economy does well, the prices rise. As the prices rise, the value of investments also rise. This is one reason people keep their investments for

THE GREAT RECESSION

Between 2008 and 2009, the United States economy took a downturn. This was called the Great Recession. Stocks fell in price. Businesses lost money when their stocks lost value. They laid off people to save money. This caused unemployment to rise. The value of houses fell. People had to pay back the amount they borrowed. People could not sell their homes for enough money. It took many years for the United States to recover.

Knowing where to invest can be tricky. Financial advisors can help people make decisions.

many years. Investments will recover as the economy recovers.

Investing may be risky. But it offers higher returns than saving alone. People talk to experts to make sure they are making smart money choices. These experts are financial advisors. They help people make the best choices for their goals. One investment website explained, "The financial advisor is also an educator. Part of the advisor's task is to help you understand what is involved in meeting your future goals."[2]

Saving and investing can seem confusing. There are many options available. That is why it is important for people to do their research. People must decide what they want from their finances in the future. After that, they can make smart money decisions.

CHAPTER TWO

WHY DO PEOPLE SAVE AND INVEST?

People save and invest for many reasons. Sometimes it is for large purchases, such as cars and houses. Other times, it is for life events. These events can include going to college or retiring. People save and invest better when they know how they want to use their money.

Most people can't afford the full price of a house, so they usually get a loan.

MAKING LARGE PURCHASES

There are many people who want or need to make large purchases. These could include a car, a vacation, or a house. These purchases can cost thousands or hundreds of thousands of dollars. Not many people have that much money lying around. People need to save and invest for several months or years.

People often use loans to pay for houses and cars. People pay the loans off over time. Home mortgages are usually fifteen- or thirty-year loans. Car loans are

THE IMPORTANCE OF A BUDGET

A budget is a person's plan for their money. It tracks income and spending. People can know if they have enough money to pay for things they need. Budgets also help plan for saving and investing. Budgets help people know how much they can afford to save each month. Budgets also help people cut costs. Then people can put more money into savings.

shorter. Many car loans last for around five years. But both of these require a buyer to pay a portion of the price up front. This is called a **down payment**. Many down payments are made in cash or checks. It is best not to put down payments on credit cards. But some people might. If they do, it is important that they can afford to pay the credit card off quickly. Credit cards have high interest rates.

People can save and invest for more than just needs. Saving and investing can also help people afford things they want, such as travel. More and more people want to travel. One study showed that today's young people travel the most out of all age groups. According to another study, young people "are more interested in spending their money on experiences rather than big purchases."[3] They may want to see the world more than they want to buy a house.

PAYING FOR COLLEGE

It is important to save for college early. College is expensive. Some families choose to start a college fund for their children. Family members can give money or savings bonds. A savings bond is sold by the government to the public. People purchase

Parents may buy savings bonds for their children. When the children grow up, the savings bonds will be worth more.

bonds for a certain value. That money goes directly to the government. The government promises to pay back the bond with interest as the bond **matures**. As the children grow up, their college fund also grows.

In 2018, most college students needed help paying for school. They had to take out loans. Student Loan Hero is a company that helps people manage their student loans. It says the class of 2018 "graduated with an average debt of $29,800."[4] That is the cost of a new car. College debt can affect young people's financial goals. They may not be able to buy a house. They might not be able to start a family. As college tuition rises, it is likely debt will also rise.

Saving for college can help lower the debt a person graduates with. Even using savings to buy textbooks can make an impact. Few people can save enough to pay all of their college expenses. But savings can help cover some costs.

PLANNING FOR RETIREMENT

Some kids start working as early as fourteen. Many people spend forty to fifty years working. Then, they retire in

SOCIAL SECURITY

The US government created Social Security in 1935. Most people know Social Security as a retirement fund. That is one of its purposes. A part of each employee's paycheck goes to Social Security. When people retire, they receive money each month. Nearly 45 million retired Americans receive these benefits.

Some people travel when they retire.

their sixties. People save and invest so they can retire. They need money saved in order to live comfortably when they retire. Retirement often allows people to do things they were not able to do when they were working. One of the biggest things is traveling.

Expenses do not stop when people retire. People need to pay for their homes, cars, and groceries. Add vacations, and retirement can become pretty expensive. People save and invest their money when they start working. This money gains interest over time. The more money that is in the account, the more money people gain in interest. Many people choose to invest their money to save for retirement. Investments may earn more than savings accounts over a long period of time.

When people retire, they can live off their investments and Social Security benefits. Social Security is money paid by the government. It goes to people who retire, become disabled, or lose a spouse.

People want to be comfortable when they retire. As people age, they are more likely to have health problems. Saving and investing can cover the costs of medical care.

PREPARING FOR THE UNEXPECTED

Unexpected events happen. The loss of a job may cause financial trouble. A broken phone may be too expensive to replace.

Insurance helps cover the cost of medical bills.

Many people rely on credit cards to pay for unexpected expenses. But experts say it is better to use savings when possible.

A trip to the hospital can cost thousands of dollars, even with insurance. Most hospitals and clinics have payment plans. People can pay their bills off over time. This can make large bills easier to handle.

People sometimes lose their jobs. That's one reason why it is important to save money.

But people still need to have the money to cover the cost. Saving money in an emergency fund can help. People can create a savings account to hold their emergency fund.

Many experts say that it is best to save three to six months' worth of expenses.

Not everyone can afford to save that much. Other experts say that even $500 will work. The amount people need depends on their living situation. For example, a family of four may need more money saved. A single person living with roommates may need less. The amount can also depend on how people plan to use savings. Savings of $500 to $1,000 can pay for unexpected expenses. These can include car repairs. But people may want to save more. They could lose their jobs. They could get sick. Saving for unexpected events can help keep people financially safe.

CHAPTER THREE

HOW DO PEOPLE SAVE MONEY?

There are many ways for people to save money. Banks have savings accounts. People can get certificates of deposit (CDs). The government offers savings bonds. These are each effective for different goals.

SAVINGS ACCOUNTS

An easy way to save money is by setting up a savings account. Banks offer savings

Some banks allow people to deposit their money using a drive-through.

accounts. These accounts are easy to set up. Some savings accounts are free. Others may charge a fee. Banks may require a small opening deposit. A deposit is an amount of money put into an account. This deposit is often around twenty-five dollars.

Banks may also require a minimum balance. This means there must always be a certain amount of money in the account. Not all banks require a minimum balance.

Setting up an account is simple. People creating an account need their ID. They may

SAVE $1,000

One thousand dollars is a lot of money. It might seem like it will take a long time to reach that goal. But it is possible to save more than $1,000 in a year. One way is to save three dollars each day. Another way is to put money away each week. Start with one dollar the first week. The second week, save two dollars. In the last week of the year, a person would save fifty-two dollars. The total the person saved that year would be $1,378.

also need personal information such as their address and Social Security number. Savings accounts are easy to maintain. Many banks also do not charge people to keep the account. They won't charge a fee so long as people add money each month. The money earns interest as long as the account is open.

Savings accounts allow people to access their money. Other saving and investing options make it more difficult to withdraw. But savings accounts make it easy. People can withdraw money at any time. Many banks also have online banking. People can

People use online banking because it's convenient.

transfer money between savings and checking accounts from home.

Easy access is important. Savings accounts help people cover the costs of emergencies. Emergencies can come up quickly. One emergency could be a health concern. Or something in the house could break. People will need their savings right away to pay for these. There are certain repairs people know will happen. But emergencies cannot be predicted. That is why savings accounts are important.

Unfortunately, many people don't have enough savings to cover an emergency. Researchers studied this in 2016. They found that "about 46 percent of Americans said they did not have enough money to cover a $400 emergency expense."[5] That rate was even higher when the cost was $500.

Most experts agree that having a savings account is important. One expert recommends having two accounts. One is an emergency fund. It covers "three to six months of living expenses." The other is a "'life happens' fund." It is "for those unexpected expenses like a major car repair."[6]

There are many pros to savings accounts. But the biggest con is low interest rates. Most do not keep up with inflation. Inflation means money loses value over time. The inflation rate is how much the price of goods goes up each year.

Inflation causes the price of goods, such as groceries, to go up.

With inflation, money cannot buy as much as it did before. In 2018, the inflation rate was 1.9 percent. But the average interest rate for savings accounts is just 0.01 percent. That means people earn just one penny for every $100 in the account.

When the interest rate is that low, a person's money loses buying power.

SAVINGS BONDS

Savings bonds are a safe option for putting money away. These bonds are loans to the government. The government then pays back the money with interest. Savings bonds have fixed interest rates. They have

COMPOUND INTEREST

Compound interest and simple interest are two types of interest for savings accounts. Simple interest is earned on the **principal**. But compound interest is earned on the total money in the account, including interest that was previously earned. The savings grow faster with compound interest.

higher interest rates than savings accounts. In 2019, the annual interest rate was 0.1 percent.

Savings bonds have a "life." A bond earns interest during its life. It stops earning interest at the end of its life. At that point, the bond is said to be mature. The life of a bond can be as long as thirty years. Savings bonds are popular gifts because of this. A person can give someone a twenty-five-dollar savings bond that will mature to much more than that.

The US government insures savings bonds. When the economy goes through a

Savings bonds help people with their long-term goals.

downturn, savings bonds won't lose money. Other investment options do.

Savings bonds are great for long-term goals. These goals can include college tuition. Savings bonds are different from savings accounts. Savings bonds don't let people easily access their money. Bonds cannot be cashed in the first year. People can cash the bond after that. But there is a penalty in the first five years. With the penalty, people lose the last three months of interest. Savings bonds earn more if they are left for long periods.

Savings bonds are taxed. When people cash their savings bonds, they must pay a tax on the interest that was earned. This tax goes back to the government.

CERTIFICATES OF DEPOSIT

Banks offer certificates of deposit. People put money into a CD. This money is called the deposit. The deposit stays there for a certain amount of time. Banks offer higher interest rates if people leave the money longer.

CDs have a lot in common with savings bonds. Like savings bonds, CDs are insured by the US government. They store money for a period of time. The original deposit is called the principal. Interest collects and compounds on the principal. When interest compounds, interest is paid on the new balance. Some accounts have interest that is only paid on the principal. Compound interest gains

The longer money is kept in a CD, the more value it will have.

money more quickly. Usually interest is paid monthly. CDs have shorter life terms than savings bonds. But people still cannot take money from the account early. If they do, it causes a penalty.

Cars cost a lot of money. People make a down payment on them and pay the rest later.

Interest rates vary based on a CD's life. A CD may have a life of three months. Another CD may have a ten-year life. A three-month CD will generally have a lower interest rate than a ten-year CD. Investors say it is a trade-off. It is much easier to wait three months to access savings. Ten years is a lot more time. But after ten years, a CD will collect a lot of interest.

CDs are often used for purchase goals. A person might know they will need a new car in three years. They can open a CD to help save for the down payment. CDs are also good for paying for big vacations. Their shorter life makes them a good choice for these types of goals.

CHAPTER FOUR

HOW DO PEOPLE INVEST MONEY?

There are many options for people who want to invest money. People invest for different reasons. Some invest to build wealth. One main reason is to set aside money for retirement. It is very difficult to live on Social Security benefits alone. People keep investments as an added cushion. But investments carry risks.

Social Security can't cover all the costs of living.

STOCK MARKET

A group of men gathered under a tree in 1792. They signed an agreement. This agreement turned into the New York Stock Exchange (NYSE). The NYSE is the

Wall Street in New York City is home to the NYSE.

largest stock exchange in the world. Many people look to the NYSE to see how the world economy is doing.

The NYSE has a list of company names. These are the companies that trade in the exchange. To trade means to buy and sell stocks. One of the ways companies raise money is by selling stocks to people. The people become shareholders in the company. As the company grows, its stock is worth more money. Shareholders can sell their stocks for more than they paid for them. This is how people make money on the stock market.

A stock exchange is a busy place. Stockbrokers used to yell out their bids to buy stocks. Today, few stockbrokers buy that way. Most use computers to trade stocks. Stockbrokers are professional investors. They often work for companies

People can use their phones to check their stocks and brokerage accounts.

or individuals. They bid on or sell stocks for their clients. The NYSE is a busy and exciting place. Buying and selling stocks can seem overwhelming. But technology is making it easier. Now, most trading happens online.

Investing in the stock market can be easy. People can use the internet to find an online brokerage. A brokerage is a company that buys and sells investments for people. A brokerage account is similar to a bank account. People can add money to this account often or rarely. The money in the account is eventually used to buy stocks and bonds.

Investors decide what companies to buy stocks from. With so many choices, this can seem impossible. But experts say to think first about companies you already know. Dayana Yochim is an expert on investing. She says, "You're looking for companies of which you want to become a part owner."[7] There are also online services that help investors choose stocks and bonds. A person sets investment goals. The online tool then chooses stocks and bonds for the investor.

There is a fee to buy stocks. This fee goes toward paying for the stockbroker's time. It is important that people read all of the requirements for the brokerage.

Some charge an upfront fee. Others say they charge nothing for trades. But these companies may charge a percentage of the investment. They charge when investors sell their shares. People may end up paying more in the end with this agreement.

INVESTING IN COMMODITIES AND REAL ESTATE

People can invest in commodities and real estate. Commodities include natural resources, such as gold and oil. Many people invest in gold because it is stable. Even if the market becomes less profitable, gold continues to be valuable. Real estate is another way to invest. People invest in property. For example, a house's value may go up. The house is then sold for a profit. The profit is the return on the investment.

People may invest in a mutual fund. Mutual funds are a collection of stocks or bonds. These funds let people invest in many stocks in one purchase. Mutual funds make it quick and easy for people to invest with less risk.

When investing, it can be helpful to talk to someone. Financial advisors help people understand what their options are.

RETIREMENT ACCOUNTS

Some experts say it is best to start saving for retirement as soon as possible. Others say it is okay to wait a while. They say it is just as important to get rid of debt.

People can save for retirement at a young age or use their income to pay off debt.

Douglas Boneparth helps people plan their finances. He thinks it is important for young people to learn how to control their spending. They should do this before

Money from retirement accounts helps cover the costs of living after people stop working.

they invest. He asks, "What good is investing if you don't know what your goals are and can't effectively save?"[8]

Retirement accounts are investments that get tax benefits. People can take money out of their accounts when they retire. This money pays for their retirement. There are two main types of retirement accounts. One is the 401(k). Businesses often offer 401(k)s. These are for employees. Employees add money to the accounts. This money comes out of their paychecks. Sometimes, employers will match what employees put into the account. They match up to a certain percentage of the employee's salary. In 2019, the average employer match for a 401(k) was around 4.5 percent. Most experts suggest people put in as much money as their employer is willing to match.

Money in a 401(k) is not taxed until it is taken out of the account.

The other retirement plan is an IRA. This stands for Individual Retirement Account. Employers may offer these accounts. But people can open an IRA without going through their employer. People invest in an

IRA as they would in a 401(k). But there is a cap. This limits how much people can put in an IRA. In 2019, the cap was about $6,000. The cap for 401(k)s is much higher. People can take money from their IRA at any time. But this money may receive a penalty. After people are fifty-nine and a half years old, they can withdraw from an IRA without a penalty. People with 401(k)s must wait until they are fifty-nine and a half years old. Before then, there are few conditions under which they can withdraw.

IRAs and 401(k)s are taxed similarly. When people put money into a 401(k), they do not pay taxes on that money. The money is taken out of their paycheck. It is deposited directly into the account. This is called a pretax contribution.

People do not have to pay taxes on the money in 401(k) accounts. However, when people decide to use their 401(k) money, then they must pay taxes. This money is income. Income is taxed by the government. These taxes fund programs like Social Security.

Like 401(k)s, IRAs have pretax contributions. Money people put into an IRA does not count as taxable income.

There are pros and cons to traditional and Roth IRAs.

When people take money from the account, they pay taxes on it.

There are also Roth accounts. These can be for IRAs and 401(k)s. The government takes taxes out of the paycheck first. Then investors put money into their accounts.

When they withdraw, no further taxes are taken. Some people prefer this method. They know how much money they have. They do not have to consider taxes when they are ready to withdraw.

Like other investment accounts, retirement investments are held in a mixture

DIVERSIFYING

Diversifying is an important part of investing. It is the process of investing in different companies and options. Some investments have high risks. Higher risks also mean higher returns. But it is not good to have only high-risk investments. Low-risk investments, such as bonds, have lower returns. But they are reliable. By diversifying, people are able to get a more reliable return on their investments.

of stocks and bonds. Bonds are less risky than stocks. There are different kinds of bonds people can invest in. Companies and local governments offer bonds. When people buy these bonds, they lend money to the company or government. The money will be paid back with interest. These bonds are much like savings bonds. But unlike savings bonds, these are not insured by the government.

BALANCING RISKS

People can choose what kinds of investments they want for their account. One person may want a risky investment.

It could sharply increase or decrease in value. These investments include more stocks. Another person may want a safer investment. It is unlikely to rise in value quickly. But it is also unlikely to drop. Some employers offer packages that are already a mix of high- and low-risk investments. These packages offer simplicity for employees.

Paying for a house, retirement, and even college can seem far away. But starting to save and invest early is important. Practicing good money skills can make a big difference later on. When emergencies

Employees receive different benefits that include options for saving and investing.

come up, it is important to have money saved to pay for them. Saving and investing are long-term skills. People of all ages can practice them.

WORKSHEET

To make sure others can use this book, please complete the activity on a separate sheet of paper.

MAKE A SAVINGS PLAN

Many people save for specific goals. Saving for a goal requires a plan. Answer the questions below to make your own savings plan. This can be for a real or an imaginary goal.

SET A GOAL

1. What are you saving for?
2. How much money do you need to save for it?

CREATE A TIMELINE

3. When will you need it? Or how long are you planning to save for it?
4. How often will you contribute to your savings?

CHOOSE A METHOD

5. How will you save? For example, will you save with a piggy bank, a savings account, or with something else like a CD or savings bond? Why did you choose that method?

6. How much money will you need to deposit each time you contribute to stay on track?

REVIEW YOUR PLAN

7. What are some ways you could save more money? How much could you add to your savings?

8. If you save more, how much more quickly will you reach your goal?

9. Can you afford the amount you need to save to meet your goal? If not, how much longer will you need to extend your timeline?

GLOSSARY

advisor
a person who gives advice

down payment
a portion of the money for a large purchase paid up front

expense
something that requires spending money

interest
money earned for keeping a deposit in an account

loans
lent money that is paid back with interest

matures
grows to its full value

penalty
a punishment in the form of a fee

principal
the original amount of money deposited into an account

tuition
the cost of a year of college

withdraw
to take out

SOURCE NOTES

CHAPTER ONE: WHAT ARE SAVING AND INVESTING?

1. Carolyn O'Hara, "How Much Money Do I Need to Retire?" *AARP the Magazine*, n.d. www.aarp.org/magazine.

2. Amy Fontinelle, "What Do Financial Advisors Do?" *Investopedia*, September 27, 2019. www.investopedia.com.

CHAPTER TWO: WHY DO PEOPLE SAVE AND INVEST?

3. Kacey Mya, "Why Millennials Have Become the Wanderlust Generation," *Travel* (blog), *US News and World Report*, February 3, 2017. https://travel.usnews.com.

4. "A Look at the Shocking Student Loan Debt Statistics for 2019," *Student Loan Hero*, February 4, 2019. https://studentloanhero.com.

CHAPTER THREE: HOW DO PEOPLE SAVE MONEY?

5. Ylan Q. Mui, "The Shocking Number of Americans Who Can't Cover a $400 Expense," *Washington Post*, May 25, 2016. www.washingtonpost.com.

6. Michell Singletary, "How Quickly Should New Graduates Start Saving for Retirement?" *Washington Post*, May 23, 2019. www.washingtonpost.com.

CHAPTER FOUR: HOW DO PEOPLE INVEST MONEY?

7. Dayana Yochim, "How to Buy Stocks," *NerdWallet*, August 28, 2019. www.nerdwallet.com.

8. Quoted in Singletary, "How Quickly Should New Graduates Start Saving for Retirement?"

FOR FURTHER RESEARCH

BOOKS

Craig E. Blohm, *Teen Guide to Credit and Debt*. San Diego, CA: ReferencePoint Press, 2017.

Stephen Currie, *Teen Guide to Saving and Investing*. San Diego, CA: ReferencePoint Press, 2017.

James McKenna, et al., *How to Turn $100 into $1,000,000*. New York: Workman Publishing, 2016.

INTERNET SOURCES

Amy Fontinelle, "Why Saving Money Is Important," *Investopedia*, July 15, 2019. www.investopedia.com.

Elizabeth Hoyt, "Money Saving Advice for College Students," *Fastweb*, August 21, 2019. www.fastweb.com.

"Not Saving? These 3 Reasons to Save Money Will Give You the Motivation to Start," *Modern Money* (blog), *Discover*, n.d. www.discover.com.

WEBSITES

TheMint

www.themint.org

This educational website teaches kids and teens about managing money and developing good financial habits.

NYSE

www.nyse.com

The New York Stock Exchange is the largest stock exchange in the world. Millions of trades happen each day.

Roth IRA

www.rothira.com

This website provides information about Roth IRA accounts.

INDEX

IMAGE CREDITS

Cover: © Billion Photos/Shutterstock Images
5: © EdBockStock/Shutterstock Images
7: © Gorodenkoff/Shutterstock Images
8: © LumiNola/iStockphoto
11: © monkeybusinessimages/iStockphoto
13: © Syda Productions/Shutterstock Images
14: © Red Line Editorial
17: © ktasimar/Shutterstock Images
20: © Prostock-studio/Shutterstock Images
23: © 4 PM production/Shutterstock Images
27: © Trum Ronnarong/Shutterstock Images
30: © adamkaz/iStockphoto
33: © everydayplus/Shutterstock Images
34: © baranq/Shutterstock Images
37: © Dominique James/Shutterstock Images
40: © Rawpixel.com/Shutterstock Images
43: © PR Image Factory/Shutterstock Images
46: © Jitalia17/iStockphoto
49: © designer491/Shutterstock Images
50: © zorandimzr/iStockphoto
53: © Andrey_Popov/Shutterstock Images
54: © Lucky-photographer/Shutterstock Images
56: © Bro Crock/Shutterstock Images
61: © Andrey_Popov/Shutterstock Images
62: © FilippoBacci/iStockphoto
64: © DNY59/iStockphoto
67: © designer491/Shutterstock Images
71: © garagestock/Shutterstock Images
73: © Andrey_Popov/Shutterstock Images

ABOUT THE AUTHOR

Martha London writes books for young readers. When she isn't writing, you can find her hiking in the woods.